TEN
PRINCIPLES

For A Life Worth Living

Practicing Spiritual Principles Daily
Through the Use of Affirmations

Ivonne,
Remember,
how much you
are loved and
adored more than
you know!

Karen Mills-Alston

Love
2/3/19

This edition is published by
That Guy's House in 2019

www.ThatGuysHouse.com

hey,

Welcome to this wonderful book brought to you by That Guy's House Publishing.

At That Guy's House we believe in real and raw wellness books that inspire the reader from a place of authenticity and honesty.

This book has been carefully crafted by both the author and publisher with the intention that it will bring you a glimmer of hope, a rush of inspiration and sensation of inner peace.

It is our hope that you thoroughly enjoy this book and pass it onto friends who may also be in need of a glimpse into their own magnificence.

Have a wonderful day.

Love,

Sean Patrick

That Guy.

This book is dedicated to my grandmother
Rubye Pettaway Turner for her courage
to break free from time, step into eternity
and rise in excellence. Generations are
awaking up. I am grateful. I love you.

This book is also dedicated to my
dear friend Joe Thomas who reminds
me daily to "rest in Thee."

TEN
PRINCIPLES

Introduction

How to Use this Book:
Practice, Practice, Practice

That which transforms your life is what you practice. And what you practice constitutes your personal laws of life—not what you merely believe in, but what you practice. It's all well and good to read books and to attend seminars, lectures and workshops and to say, "Oh, that really resonates with me! It's now part of my life's philosophy." Your philosophy may give you a temporary state of euphoria, but if you want to be anchored in Reality, it takes practice, practice, practice. We are not here to be euphoric but to get free. Rudimentary spirituality is theory; advanced spirituality is practice. What you practice, you ultimately embody, paving the way for breakthroughs, insight, fresh realizations and the evolutions of consciousness. In truth, that which is inconceivable is caught and understood by those who are making their spiritual practices a way of life.

Michael Bernard Beckwith
Spiritual Liberation

What practice do you have in place when stuff hits the fan, you are triggered and spiraling down the rabbit hole? Joel S. Goldsmith states that human beings are like pendulums allowing thoughts to be swayed by whatever is in the air…."If optimism, boom and prosperity are in the air, you feel inflated. If there is infection and contagion in the air, the first thing you know, you have flu or grippe." He goes on to say "… it has been demonstrated that those who are willing to take the driver's seat in their minds and govern their own thinking, who decide what they wish to think and for how long a time they wish to think it, those people have some dominion over their lives." Goldsmith's point? "You govern your surroundings by the nature of what is taking place in your consciousness."

The practice of taking dominion over your thoughts, creating a life worth living (I believe) begins with affirmations. An affirmation is a statement of Truth about the Presence, the Universe, love, peace, harmony, etc. Such is changeless, absolute and eternal. Because we are individualized expressions of this Presence, that which is True about IT is True about each of us. These Truths are realized in our consciousness through practice. We soon make them our "go to" response when stuff hits the fan and with embodiment, we are no longer at the impulse of our human nature. We remember to return to the center of our being! We are free!

I have had a practice of using affirmations since I was fifteen years old. I know how affirmations can lift my consciousness when I feel as though I am stuck in the muck and mire of life. The idea is not to stay stuck! We get to "wake up quicker" as Reverend Kathleen McNamara suggests. Thus the power of affirmations.

Here's my suggestion to use this book and the affirmations therein: Choose one affirmation each day or even week to allow for the expansion of your Spiritual Practice. Close your eyes, take a conscious breath and read the chosen affirmation out loud. Hear it and feel it vibrationally match your Soul. Let this affirmation be the reminder of the tone you are choosing to set for your day or your week. Carry this book with you. Read the affirmation every hour on the hour. As you retire to bed, take a breath, read it out loud and give thanks for this new practice. Repeat until the affirmation flows from your heart as you become consciously aware that this affirmation is affirming who you Really are. Choose to make affirmations a consistent Spiritual Practice and be ready to experience Life that is beyond your wildest imaginings!

Peace and joy AS this practice!
Karen Mills-Alston, ALSP

I BEGIN NOW

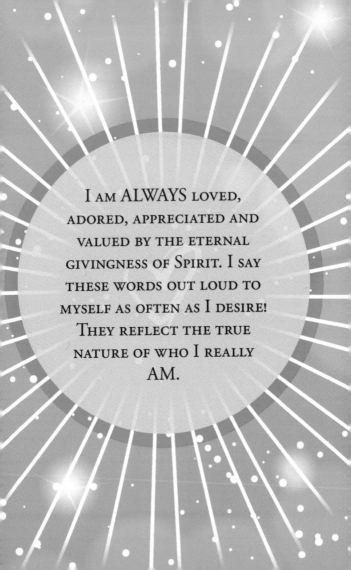

I AM ALWAYS loved, adored, appreciated and valued by the eternal givingness of Spirit. I say these words out loud to myself as often as I desire! They reflect the true nature of who I really AM.

I AM LISTENING AND SAYING YES TO MY HIGHEST GOOD REVEALING ITSELF NOW!

I NO LONGER WALK IN
LOCKSTEP WITH MEDIOCRITY.
I STEP OUT OF MY COMFORT
ZONE EXPRESSING MY UNIQUE
SELF. I WELCOME EXCELLENCE
IN ALL THINGS AS MY NEW WAY
OF BEING. I EXPERIENCE LIFE
AS LIMITLESS, BOUNDLESS,
INEXHAUSTIBLE, AND
PLENTIFUL.

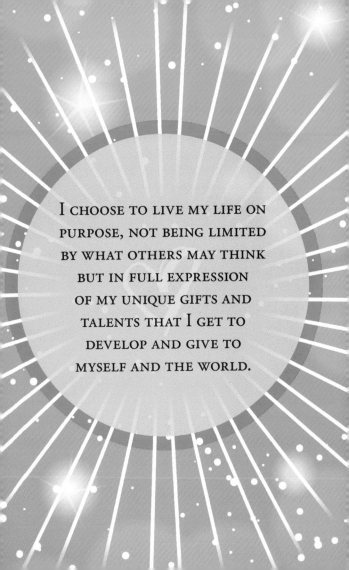

I CHOOSE TO LIVE MY LIFE ON
PURPOSE, NOT BEING LIMITED
BY WHAT OTHERS MAY THINK
BUT IN FULL EXPRESSION
OF MY UNIQUE GIFTS AND
TALENTS THAT I GET TO
DEVELOP AND GIVE TO
MYSELF AND THE WORLD.

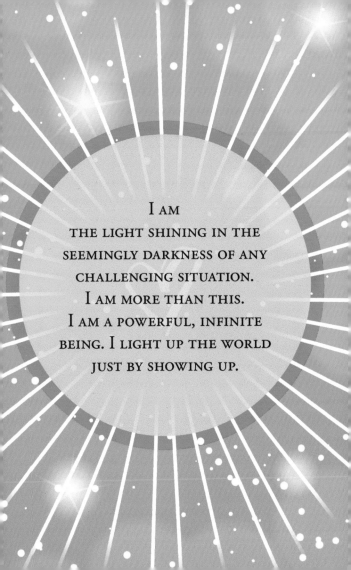

I AM
THE LIGHT SHINING IN THE
SEEMINGLY DARKNESS OF ANY
CHALLENGING SITUATION.
I AM MORE THAN THIS.
I AM A POWERFUL, INFINITE
BEING. I LIGHT UP THE WORLD
JUST BY SHOWING UP.

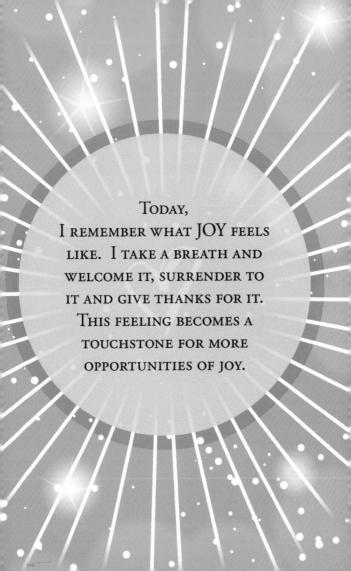

TODAY,
I REMEMBER WHAT JOY FEELS
LIKE. I TAKE A BREATH AND
WELCOME IT, SURRENDER TO
IT AND GIVE THANKS FOR IT.
THIS FEELING BECOMES A
TOUCHSTONE FOR MORE
OPPORTUNITIES OF JOY.

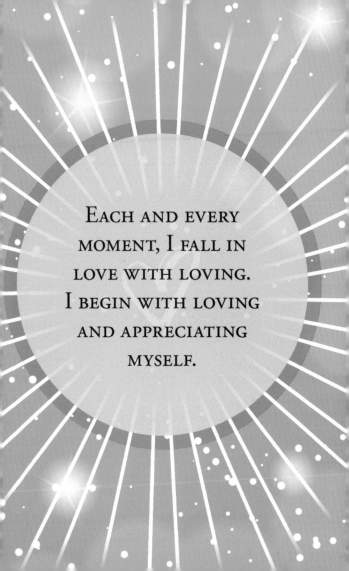

EACH AND EVERY
MOMENT, I FALL IN
LOVE WITH LOVING.
I BEGIN WITH LOVING
AND APPRECIATING
MYSELF.

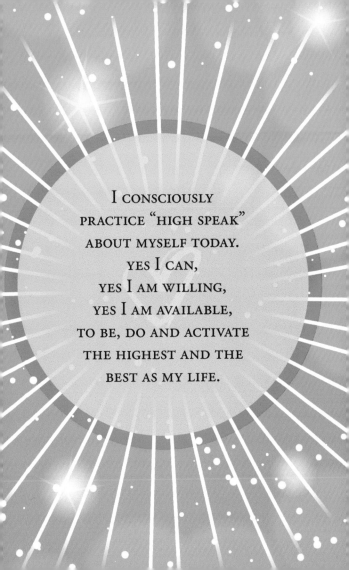

I CONSCIOUSLY
PRACTICE "HIGH SPEAK"
ABOUT MYSELF TODAY.
YES I CAN,
YES I AM WILLING,
YES I AM AVAILABLE,
TO BE, DO AND ACTIVATE
THE HIGHEST AND THE
BEST AS MY LIFE.

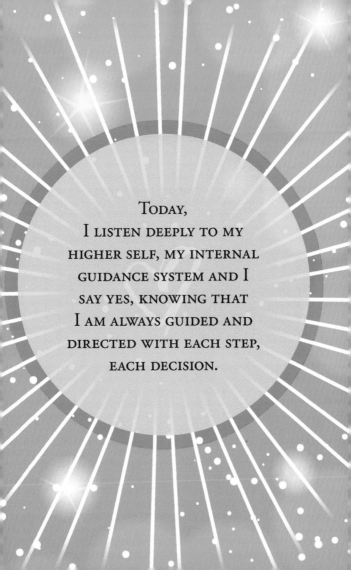

TODAY,
I LISTEN DEEPLY TO MY
HIGHER SELF, MY INTERNAL
GUIDANCE SYSTEM AND I
SAY YES, KNOWING THAT
I AM ALWAYS GUIDED AND
DIRECTED WITH EACH STEP,
EACH DECISION.

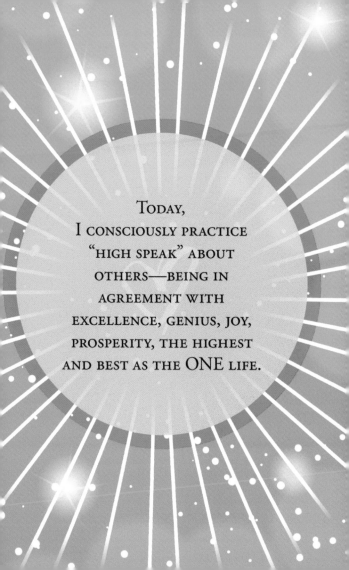

TODAY,
I CONSCIOUSLY PRACTICE
"HIGH SPEAK" ABOUT
OTHERS—BEING IN
AGREEMENT WITH
EXCELLENCE, GENIUS, JOY,
PROSPERITY, THE HIGHEST
AND BEST AS THE ONE LIFE.

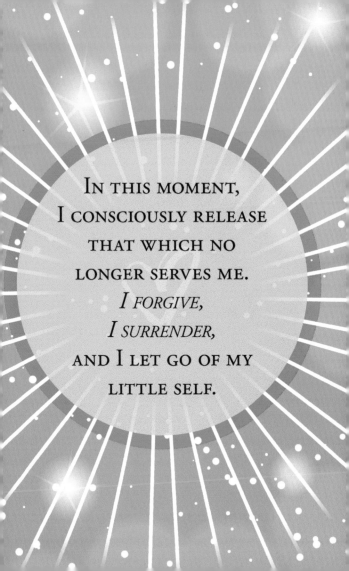

IN THIS MOMENT,
I CONSCIOUSLY RELEASE
THAT WHICH NO
LONGER SERVES ME.
I FORGIVE,
I SURRENDER,
AND I LET GO OF MY
LITTLE SELF.

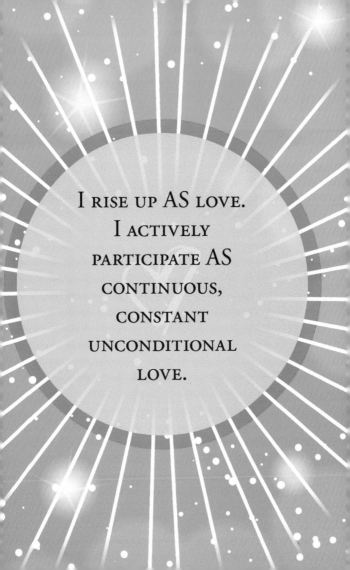

I RISE UP AS LOVE.
I ACTIVELY
PARTICIPATE AS
CONTINUOUS,
CONSTANT
UNCONDITIONAL
LOVE.

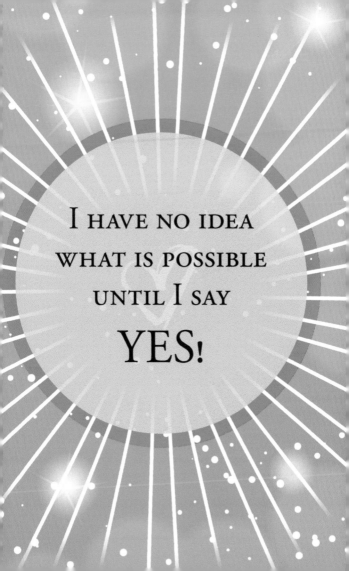

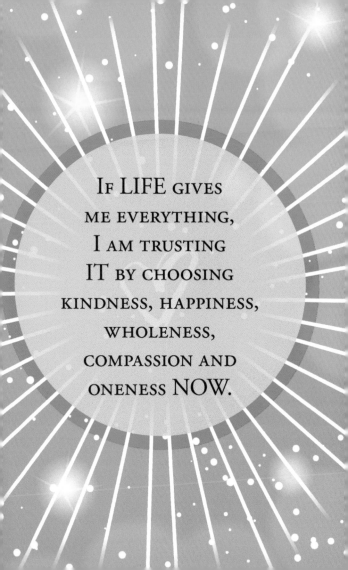

If LIFE gives
me everything,
I am trusting
IT by choosing
kindness, happiness,
wholeness,
compassion and
oneness NOW.

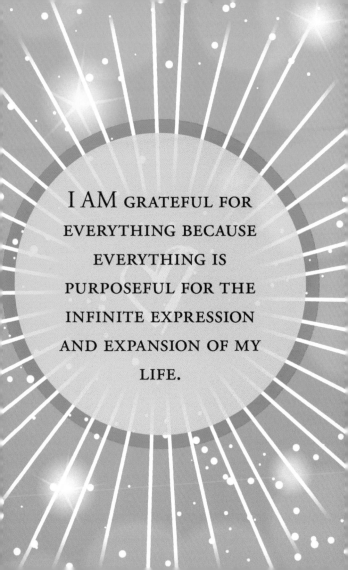

I AM GRATEFUL FOR EVERYTHING BECAUSE EVERYTHING IS PURPOSEFUL FOR THE INFINITE EXPRESSION AND EXPANSION OF MY LIFE.

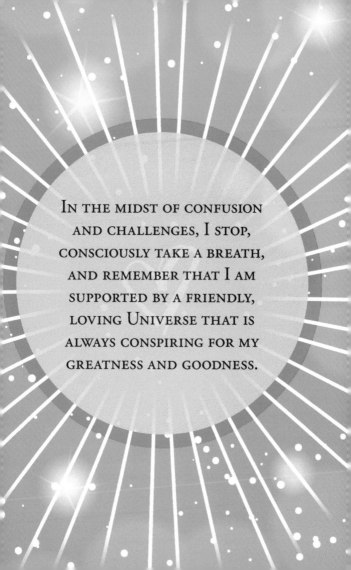

IN THE MIDST OF CONFUSION
AND CHALLENGES, I STOP,
CONSCIOUSLY TAKE A BREATH,
AND REMEMBER THAT I AM
SUPPORTED BY A FRIENDLY,
LOVING UNIVERSE THAT IS
ALWAYS CONSPIRING FOR MY
GREATNESS AND GOODNESS.

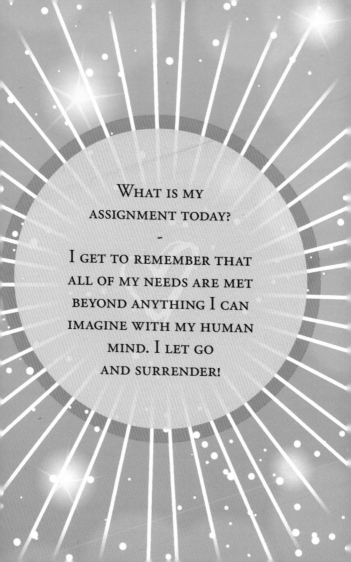

WHAT IS MY
ASSIGNMENT TODAY?
-
I GET TO REMEMBER THAT
ALL OF MY NEEDS ARE MET
BEYOND ANYTHING I CAN
IMAGINE WITH MY HUMAN
MIND. I LET GO
AND SURRENDER!

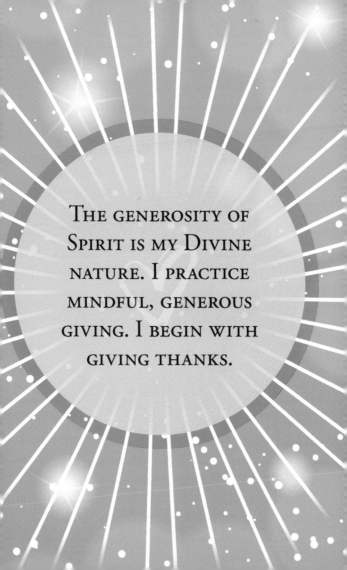

THE GENEROSITY OF
SPIRIT IS MY DIVINE
NATURE. I PRACTICE
MINDFUL, GENEROUS
GIVING. I BEGIN WITH
GIVING THANKS.

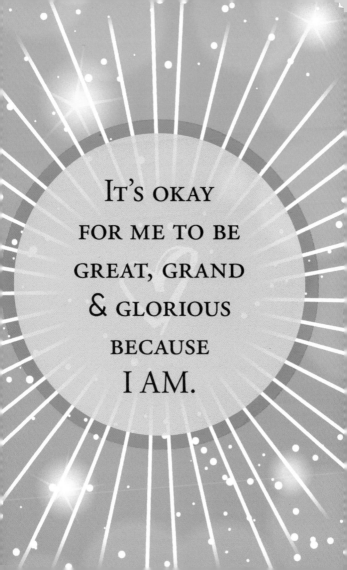

IT'S OKAY
FOR ME TO BE
GREAT, GRAND
& GLORIOUS
BECAUSE
I AM.

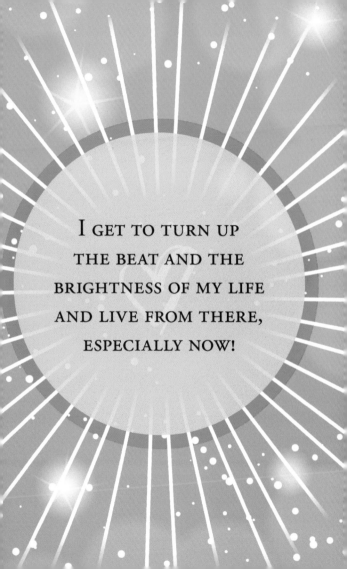

I GET TO TURN UP
THE BEAT AND THE
BRIGHTNESS OF MY LIFE
AND LIVE FROM THERE,
ESPECIALLY NOW!

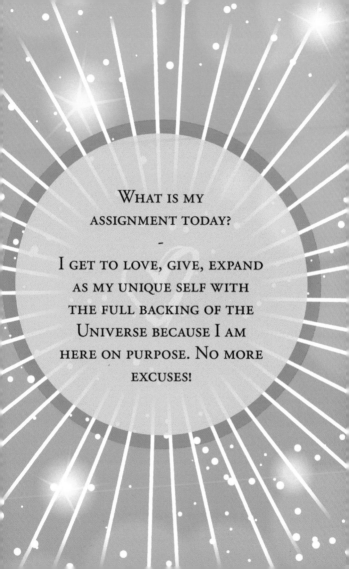

WHAT IS MY
ASSIGNMENT TODAY?
-
I GET TO LOVE, GIVE, EXPAND
AS MY UNIQUE SELF WITH
THE FULL BACKING OF THE
UNIVERSE BECAUSE I AM
HERE ON PURPOSE. NO MORE
EXCUSES!

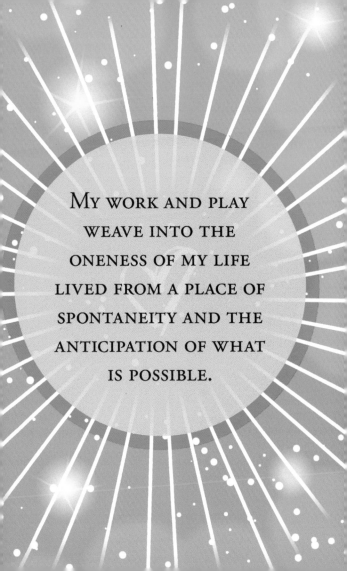

My work and play weave into the oneness of my life lived from a place of spontaneity and the anticipation of what is possible.

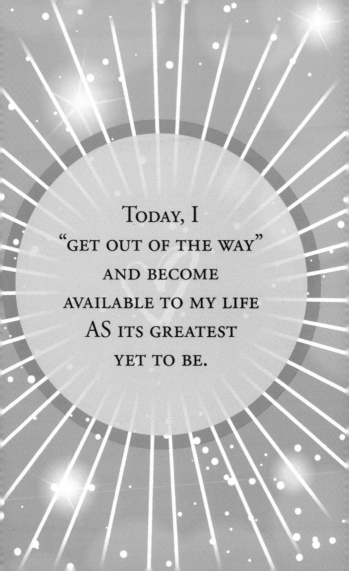

Today, I
"get out of the way"
and become
available to my life
as its greatest
yet to be.

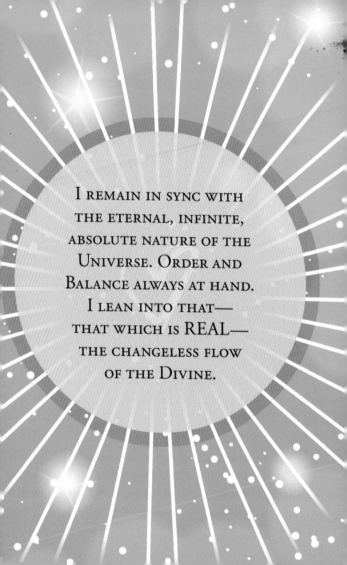

I REMAIN IN SYNC WITH
THE ETERNAL, INFINITE,
ABSOLUTE NATURE OF THE
UNIVERSE. ORDER AND
BALANCE ALWAYS AT HAND.
I LEAN INTO THAT—
THAT WHICH IS REAL—
THE CHANGELESS FLOW
OF THE DIVINE.

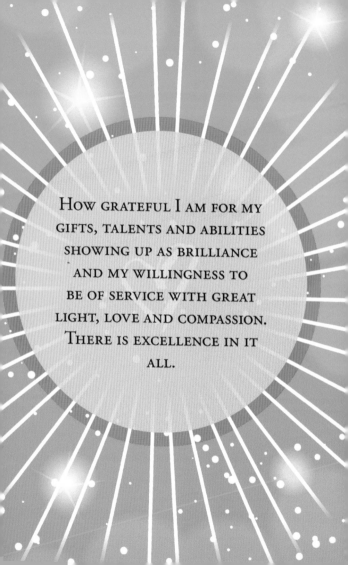

HOW GRATEFUL I AM FOR MY GIFTS, TALENTS AND ABILITIES SHOWING UP AS BRILLIANCE AND MY WILLINGNESS TO BE OF SERVICE WITH GREAT LIGHT, LOVE AND COMPASSION. THERE IS EXCELLENCE IN IT ALL.

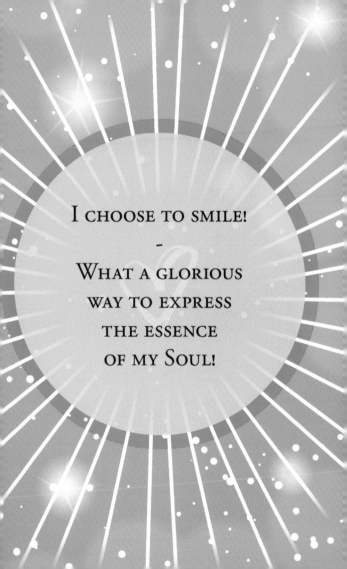

I CHOOSE TO SMILE!

-

WHAT A GLORIOUS
WAY TO EXPRESS
THE ESSENCE
OF MY SOUL!

I AM SOURCED, FUELED & SUPPLIED BY THE UNIVERSE NOW.

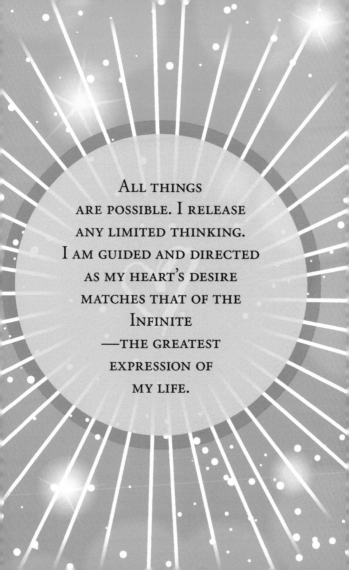

ALL THINGS
ARE POSSIBLE. I RELEASE
ANY LIMITED THINKING.
I AM GUIDED AND DIRECTED
AS MY HEART'S DESIRE
MATCHES THAT OF THE
INFINITE
—THE GREATEST
EXPRESSION OF
MY LIFE.

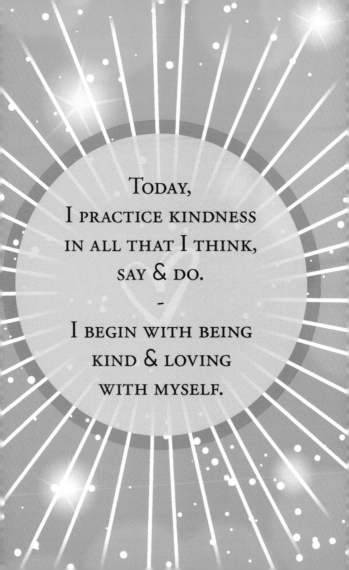

TODAY,
I PRACTICE KINDNESS
IN ALL THAT I THINK,
SAY & DO.

-

I BEGIN WITH BEING
KIND & LOVING
WITH MYSELF.

I SEE GOODNESS
EVERYWHERE I GO.
I SILENTLY BLESS EVERYONE
I SEE. I AM IN PERFECT
ALIGNMENT WITH PERFECT
IDEAS, SEEING AND FEELING
THE HIGHEST AND BEST
IN AND AS
EVERYTHING.

LOVE UNITES US.
I STAND IN THIS
DIVINE FIELD THAT
UNIFIES THE PLANET
INDIVIDUALLY
AND COLLECTIVELY.

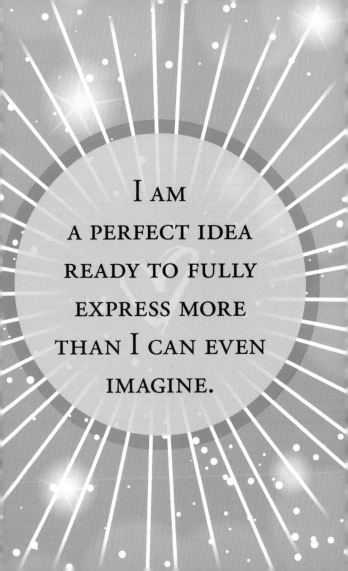

I AM
A PERFECT IDEA
READY TO FULLY
EXPRESS MORE
THAN I CAN EVEN
IMAGINE.

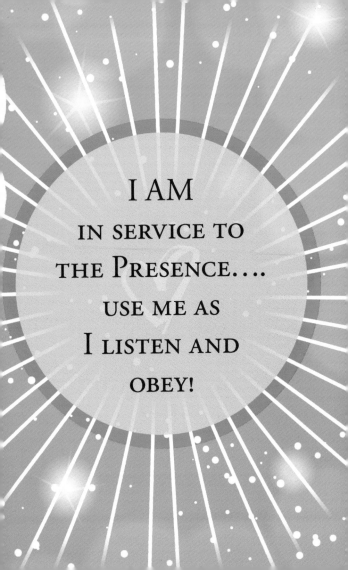

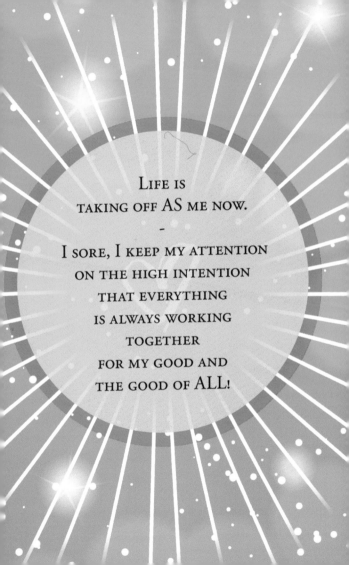

LIFE IS
TAKING OFF AS ME NOW.
-
I SORE, I KEEP MY ATTENTION
ON THE HIGH INTENTION
THAT EVERYTHING
IS ALWAYS WORKING
TOGETHER
FOR MY GOOD AND
THE GOOD OF ALL!

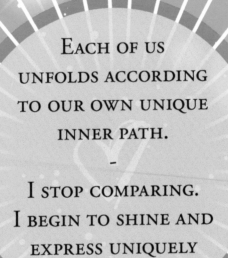

EACH OF US
UNFOLDS ACCORDING
TO OUR OWN UNIQUE
INNER PATH.

-

I STOP COMPARING.
I BEGIN TO SHINE AND
EXPRESS UNIQUELY
AS ME!

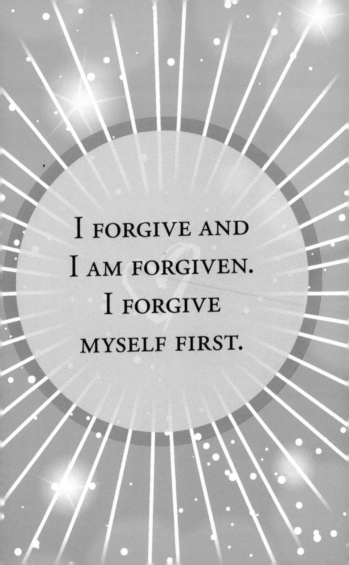

APPRECIATION
IS THE PURE
EXPRESSION OF
THE HEART.
NOTHING IS
TOO SMALL TO
APPRECIATE.

PERFECTION
IS ALWAYS
UNFOLDING.
-
I GET
TO LET IT!

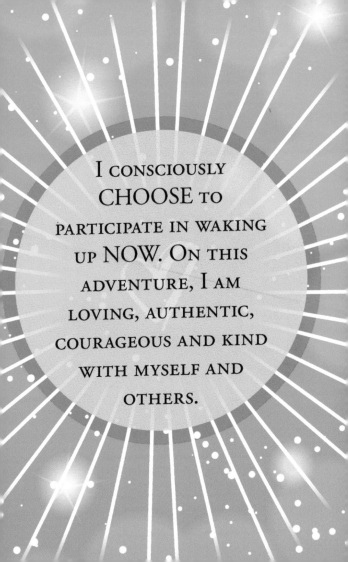

I CONSCIOUSLY
CHOOSE TO
PARTICIPATE IN WAKING
UP **NOW**. ON THIS
ADVENTURE, I AM
LOVING, AUTHENTIC,
COURAGEOUS AND KIND
WITH MYSELF AND
OTHERS.

SPIRIT WANTS
TO EXPRESS
ITSELF FULLY AND
UNIQUELY
AS ME.
-
I LET IT!

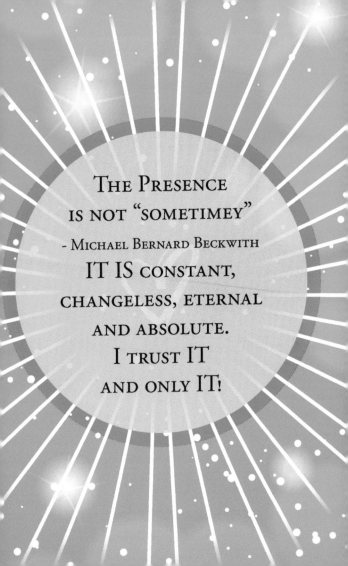

THE PRESENCE
IS NOT "SOMETIMEY"
- MICHAEL BERNARD BECKWITH
IT IS CONSTANT,
CHANGELESS, ETERNAL
AND ABSOLUTE.
I TRUST IT
AND ONLY IT!

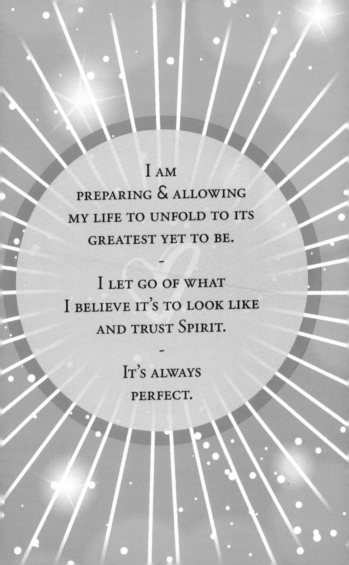

I AM
PREPARING & ALLOWING
MY LIFE TO UNFOLD TO ITS
GREATEST YET TO BE.

-

I LET GO OF WHAT
I BELIEVE IT'S TO LOOK LIKE
AND TRUST SPIRIT.

-

IT'S ALWAYS
PERFECT.

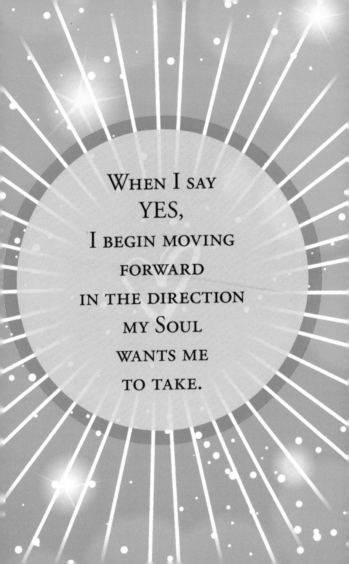

WHEN I SAY
YES,
I BEGIN MOVING
FORWARD
IN THE DIRECTION
MY SOUL
WANTS ME
TO TAKE.

WITH EVERY BEAT OF MY HEART, I AM OPEN TO CHANGE. I AM FLEXIBLE, RECEPTIVE AND TEACHABLE. I AM AVAILABLE TO CHANGE, TO EXPAND, TO UP LEVEL NOW!

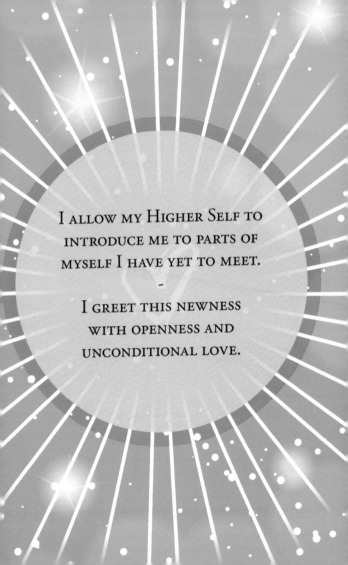

I ALLOW MY HIGHER SELF TO
INTRODUCE ME TO PARTS OF
MYSELF I HAVE YET TO MEET.

-

I GREET THIS NEWNESS
WITH OPENNESS AND
UNCONDITIONAL LOVE.

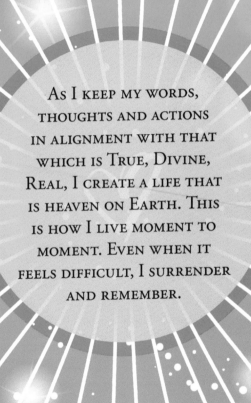

As I keep my words, thoughts and actions in alignment with that which is True, Divine, Real, I create a life that is heaven on Earth. This is how I live moment to moment. Even when it feels difficult, I surrender and remember.

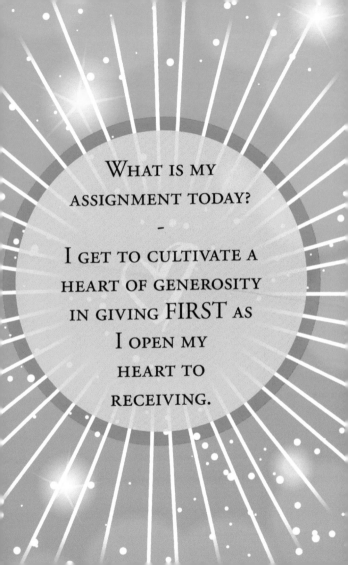

WHAT IS MY
ASSIGNMENT TODAY?
-
I GET TO CULTIVATE A
HEART OF GENEROSITY
IN GIVING FIRST AS
I OPEN MY
HEART TO
RECEIVING.

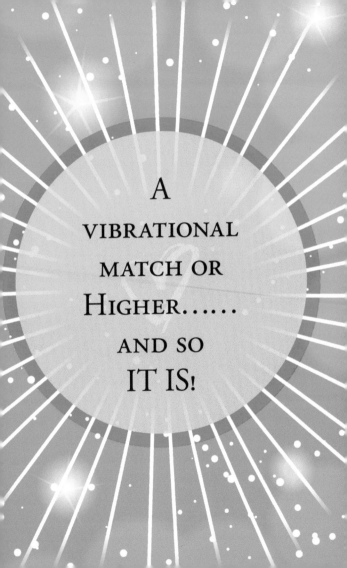

A
VIBRATIONAL
MATCH OR
HIGHER......
AND SO
IT IS!

CHANGE MAY
OFTEN FEEL
DIFFICULT.
I AM OPEN
AND FLEXIBLE
TO CHANGE
ANYWAY.

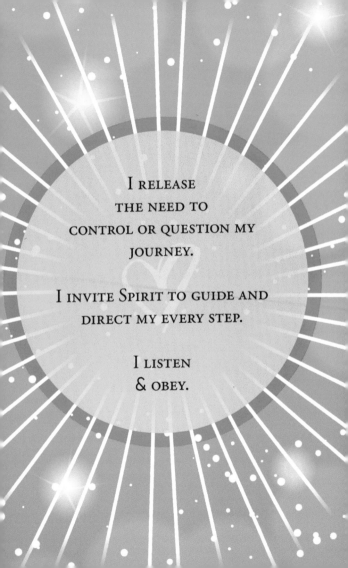

I RELEASE
THE NEED TO
CONTROL OR QUESTION MY
JOURNEY.

I INVITE SPIRIT TO GUIDE AND
DIRECT MY EVERY STEP.

I LISTEN
& OBEY.

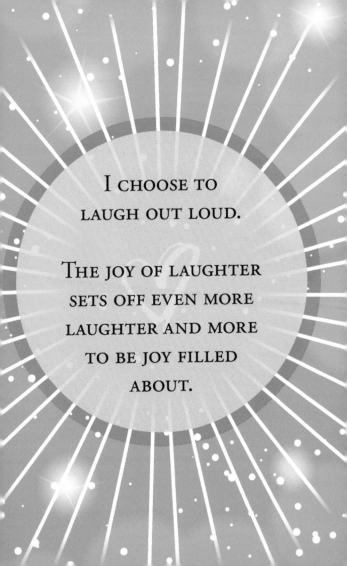

I CHOOSE TO
LAUGH OUT LOUD.

THE JOY OF LAUGHTER
SETS OFF EVEN MORE
LAUGHTER AND MORE
TO BE JOY FILLED
ABOUT.

I BEGIN AGAIN

TEN
PRINCIPLES

About the Author

A daughter and granddaughter of practitioners in the New Thought-Ageless Wisdom tradition of spirituality, Karen Mills-Alston has literally been on her spiritual path since childhood. In *10 Principles for a Life Worth Living*, she now shares the rich legacy of three generations of women who have devoted their lives to spiritual principles and practices, and proving their practical application in their lives.

After graduating from the University of Southern California with a degree in political science, Karen soon became a lobbyist for the City of Los Angeles, where she influenced municipal legislation, an experience that nourished her humanitarian impetus to positively impact the larger community and society as a whole. She later lobbied for the Airport Transport Association, along with being the Regional Government Vice President for Alaska Airlines and Southwest Airlines, respectively.

In time, Karen became the wife and CAO to one of the most well known motivational speakers, John W. Alston, until he passed away in 2011. 10 Principles for a Life Worth Living is her tribute to their mutual commitment and work of assisting individuals in actualizing their calling in life, grounded in immutable spiritual principles and practices. Of their adult daughter, Lindsay, Karen says, "Every day she reminds me of how easy it is to love. And it is that spirit of love I offer to my readers in this book."

Today, Karen serves on the Agape International Spiritual Center's Board of Trustees. She is also a member of its Leadership Team, a coordinator for Agape Ministries, an instructor in Agape's Practitioner One Student Studies, and Director of Agape's annual Revelation Conference. As an Agape Licensed Spiritual Practitioner (ALSP), she has a robust clientele that enthusiastically studies and practices the teachings found in *10 Principles for a Life Worth Living.*

The heart used throughout this
book is the symbol of the Agape
International Spiritual Center.